Animals of God

Volume Two

Also by Susan Peek

Novels for Young Adults:

Saint Magnus, The Last Viking

Crusader King

A Soldier Surrenders: The Conversion of St. Camillus de Lellis

For Children:

Animals of God, Volume One

For new titles visit www.susanpeekauthor.com

Also by Martina Parnelli:

For Children:

Fat John, His Little Lamb, and the Two Wise Owls

Coming Soon:

Little Runty, The Luckiest Donkey

Animals of God, Volume Two

Stories by Susan Peek
Illustrated by Martina Parnelli

Copyright © 2016 Susan Peek. All rights reserved.

Seven Swords Publications
ISBN-13: 978-0-9970005-3-5

Cover and Artwork © Jean Kenney

Audio rights owned exclusively by Regina Martyrum Productions

For ordering information, please contact:
SevenSwordsPublications@gmail.com
www.susanpeekauthor.com

S.P. - Dedicated to Saint Anne, the perfect Grandmother,
and to my beautiful grandchildren.

M.P — The Illustrator dedicates this volume to Saint Michael the Archangel
and to her own dear guardian angel,
with gratitude for their assistance and protection.

TABLE OF CONTENTS

THE LION WHO LOST HIS APPETITE

CUTHBERT FOR BREAKFAST

BONUS: Reproducible Coloring Pages in Back!

THE LION WHO LOST HIS APPETITE

Chapter One

Not Fed . . . and Fed UP!

The very moment Leonie the Lioness awoke that morning, she could tell that her husband was in a bad mood again. He was pacing back and forth in their cage, his tail drooping to the ground, a sullen expression on his face. Leonie stretched, stood up, and walked to where he was standing by the bars of the cage. "Rex, what's the matter?" she asked sleepily.

The big lion turned to face her. "What's the matter!" he growled. "What do you mean, what's the matter? Everything's the matter! To start with, I'm hungry and I want my breakfast!"

"But, dear, it's too early for breakfast," Leonie said patiently. "The lion-keeper won't be coming until the sun is higher up in the sky. You should know that by now. He always comes when the sun is right *there* -- just above that row of benches." Leonie pointed through the bars of the cage with one of her huge paws. "It's no use getting upset about it. That won't make him come any quicker."

"Hmmph!" Rex said angrily. "I hate this cage. I hate everything about it. If those people had left us in the jungle where we belong, then I wouldn't have to WAIT for my breakfast every day! I would simply go out and hunt it for myself, like in the good old days!"

Leonie sighed. "I know," she agreed quietly. "I miss the jungle too. But it's not all that bad here."

"Yes it is!" her husband snapped. "Hunting! That's what I miss the most! The feeling, Leonie -- the *feeling* of stalking another animal . . . of sneaking up behind it and pouncing on it when it least suspects!" His voice was growing excited with the memory. "Being able to rip it apart, tear it limb from limb with my claws, and taste its blood as it writhes in pain and --"

"But the men *do* let us do all that, Rex," Leonie interrupted. "That's the very reason they brought us here in the first place. To kill humans."

"Oh I know, I know," Rex grumbled. "But it's been so long! And besides, there's no sport in it."

"Don't be silly, dear. It was only three days ago that they set you loose and let you kill that man. You know, the one that was the thief

and the murderer."

Only three days ago? It seemed a lot longer ago to Rex than that. He asked, "Are you sure, Leonie?"

"Of course I'm sure," she answered. "You're just too impatient, dear. That's all."

The two lions stared out the bars at the huge arena in front of them. It was in the shape of a big circle, surrounded by rows and rows of benches, where thousands of people came to sit and watch whenever the lions were set loose to kill someone.

"Humans are strange creatures," Leonie said pensively as she gazed out over the arena. "They not only kill their own kind, but they come in crowds to watch and cheer each time some poor prisoner is put to death. It's like a game to them. Look -- you can still see the bloodstains on the ground over there from the last man you ate. They hardly even bother to clean it up."

"Yeah, I don't understand people either. They're too complicated. Anyhow, it's not our problem. It they wanna come all the way to the jungle, go through the hassle of capturing us, and bring us here for the sole purpose of letting us kill *other* people, well, that's their business.

I don't care, as long as I get fed!"

Leonie said excitedly, "Speaking of getting fed, Rex, look! Here comes the lion-keeper now."

Sure enough, the familiar figure of the man was approaching in the distance, pulling his little wagon which held the lions' food and clean straw for the day. Both Rex and Leonie started to paw at the dirt and twitch their tails expectantly. When the man arrived, Rex, as usual, let out his most ferocious roar and bared his giant teeth. He loved to frighten the poor man, who almost always lost his balance or dropped the pitchfork in fear.

"S-steady, ol' fella," the man stammered, as he cautiously came closer to the cage. "I'm j-just bringing your cl-clean straw to l-lay on."

Leonie whispered, "Rex! Must you scare him like that all the time?"

"But it's *fun*," Rex answered as he reached through the bars and swiped at the man. "I like scaring people."

With trembling hands, the lion-keeper scooped some straw out of the wagon and, keeping his distance as much as possible, tossed it into the cage with his pitchfork. "There, boy . . . b-back! Back!" he

said nervously as Rex continued to claw at him through the bars.

"I wish he wouldn't call me that all the time!" Rex complained to Leonie. Then he let out another huge roar.

"Rex . . . I don't see any food in his wagon. Do you?"

Come to think of it, no. Rex didn't either.

Leonie asked, "Do you think he forgot our breakfast?"

But before Rex could answer her, the man spoke. "No m-meat for you two this morning. You'll be eating l-later." Then he tried to laugh, nervously. "Something different on today's menu."

Rex and Leonie looked at each other.

That could only mean one thing.

Suddenly excited, Rex asked, "Are you thinking what I'm thinking, Leonie?"

She said, "I think I am!"

And together they both blurted, "A *man!*"

Unable to contain his joy, Rex started to sing, "They're gonna let us eat a man! They're gonna let us eat a man!"

And in his delight, he even forgot to growl one last time at the departing lion-keeper.

Chapter Two

A Dispute Over Breakfast

The next few hours seemed to fly by for the two lions. Although hungry, their spirits were high as they waited with excitement for the upcoming event. Leonie kept busy licking and cleaning her fur; she wanted to look her best when the time came for her appearance in the arena.

"How do I look?" she asked for the seventh time.

"Fine, dear," Rex assured her, also for the seventh time. "No, wait . . . you've got a whisker out of place . . . There, that's better now."

As for himself, Rex had spent the better part of the morning practicing his meanest growls and doing some warm-up pounces. "Does this sound scary enough?" he asked, letting out a tremendous roar.

Leonie nodded with admiration. "It's perfect, dear. Simply blood curdling. If I weren't your wife, you'd scare me to death."

"Good," Rex said, satisfied with himself. "Just what I wanted to hear."

"Oh Rex, look!" Leonie exclaimed. "The humans are starting to come!"

At first it was only a few people, trickling into the benches, but soon more and more began to arrive. Men, women, children. Young, old, rich and poor -- it seemed as if the entire city was cramming themselves into the arena. As the lions watched, throngs of people pushed and shoved at each other, fighting for the best seats, shouting and laughing and cheering, and making the most amazing din.

Rex could feel his muscles twitching with anticipation. "I've never seen a crowd this big," he said. "I don't know what man we're going to kill, but he must be someone awfully important."

"Maybe he's a murderer," Leonie said. "Like the last one."

Rex grinned. "Yeah . . . he was fun. I like a guy who puts up a good fight. He actually tried to wrestle with me! As if he had a chance in the world. Hah!"

Leonie said, "Well, at least he didn't just stand there and scream, like that other man did last week. If there is one thing I can't stand, it's a coward."

"Me too," Rex agreed.

Just then, the sound of trumpets could be heard at the far end of the arena, announcing the arrival of the governor. The lions had learned that the governor was the man in charge of all this. They saw him raise one arm in the air to signal for silence, and in a few moments a great hush fell over the crowd.

The governor loudly spoke:

"People of Antioch! We have assembled here today to witness a most -- shall we say -- interesting event." He gave an evil chuckle. "At the request of our close friend, the governor of Iconium, we have agreed to put to death a citizen of his city. This criminal has been sentenced to death on the odious and terrible charge of claiming to be . . . a Christian!"

A murmur of shocked disapproval rippled through the crowd.

The governor went on. "The officials of the city of Iconium have already attempted to burn this despicable Christian at the stake, but, alas, the flames mysteriously went out before death occurred. Therefore it has been decided that the criminal shall be thrown to the lions and be eaten alive."

A great cheer went up from the crowd.

Rex started to claw at the bars of the cage. "Get on with it, man! Get on with it!" he grumbled impatiently.

Leonie was likewise bursting with excitement. "They're opening the door to the arena now," she told her husband eagerly. "I can see the criminal. Here he comes now . . ." But she didn't finish her sentence, because both lions froze in surprise at what they saw.

It was not a man who stepped into the arena. It was a beautiful young woman!

Leonie gasped in astonishment. "A lady! How . . . how very strange! They've never fed us a lady before. No wonder so many people have come to watch."

"Hmm," Rex said, licking his chops, "I wonder if a lady tastes as good as a man? Not as much meat, no doubt, but perhaps a little less chewy. What do you think, Leonie?"

"Well, I'll let you be the first to sample her, dear," Leonie answered loyally. "They'll probably let only one of us out of the cage to begin with, so the privilege can be yours."

"Thank you, Leonie my dear. You're too good of a wife! And a

privilege it will be too. A woman indeed!"

As the two lions watched, the beautiful girl walked calmly to the middle of the arena. To their surprise, she looked peaceful and happy, not at all scared as their other victims always were.

"Ladies and gentlemen," the governor mockingly announced, "behold . . . the Christian virgin, Thecla!"

Chapter Three

Thecla

The crowd went wild with jeers and shouts, but the lady named Thecla hardly seemed to notice. She knelt down in the dirt and, lifting her eyes to Heaven, made the Sign of the Cross.

Rex stomped at the ground. "Open the door!" he growled. "I've been waiting for my breakfast all day! Can't you stupid people see that I'm hungry?"

But, to Rex's great frustration, the cage door did not open. Instead, a murmur was heard from the crowd. Faint at first, but then it got louder:

"Let her go!" someone yelled. "Set the girl free!"

Other people joined in. "She's only a child! Let her go! Let her go!"

It soon became a chant from the crowd: "Let her go! Let her go!"

But, compared to the size of the crowd, it was only a small and quiet chant.

Then someone else shouted, "No! She's a witch! To the lions with her!"

Another chant arose from the crowd. "To the lions! To the lions!"

The people were screaming back and forth at each other. The uproar was getting louder and louder.

"Kill her! Kill the Christian!"

"Let her go! She's innocent!"

"Send out the lions! The Christian to the lions!"

Rex couldn't believe his ears. "Hey!" he fumed. "Wait just a minute here! This is *my* breakfast you're talkin' about! You crazy people have no right to argue about MY BREAKFAST!" He let out a tremendous roar. "Open this cage before I *break* the door down!"

Both lions heard the sound of blaring trumpets as the officials tried to silence the screaming crowd. Slowly, slowly, the shouts and arguing died down.

Leonie by now was holding her breath. "Rex, dear, listen. The governor is about to make his decision. Shhh."

"Ladies and gentlemen," the governor announced loudly. "The sentence has *already* been passed upon this maiden. She is a Christian -- a traitor -- and must be dealt with accordingly. LET THE LION FREE!"

His words were met with more shouts from the crowd, some cheering, some booing, everyone making such a racket. Suddenly the door of the cage was unbolted from above and flung open, just wide enough for one lion to pass through. Without wasting a second, Rex sprang out into the arena and let out his most ferocious roar.

"Have fun!" Leonie called to him, as the cage door slammed shut again, locking her in. "And save some for me!"

Rex called back, "You know I will, dear. I always do."

Then he charged into the arena.

The virgin Thecla rose from her knees and stood to face Rex, as his huge muscular body came pounding across the arena straight at her. A faint whisper escaped her trembling lips, "Oh Jesus, my sweet Savior! I beg of Thee the grace to be brave! Help me accept this terrible death for love of Thee. Please dear Lord, courage! Give me Thy courage . . ."

Rex slid to a stop a few feet away from Thecla. "Ah hah!" he laughed to himself. "So she's pretending to be brave, I see. Well, fine then. I'll let her have some fun at being brave." He shook his mane and bared his enormous teeth. Then he began to prance in a circle around the praying maiden, crouching down every few minutes as if he were about to pounce on her. He pawed the ground, roared, did all his usual tricks to terrify her.

But, to his growing annoyance, the young lady didn't seem afraid of him. She stood, perfectly still, her hands folded and her eyes half closed in prayer. She didn't start to scream, or cry, or go hysterical like they always did in the end. She didn't even try to run! In fact, she didn't do *anything* Rex was expecting her to do! She simply stood there, waiting, with peace.

A wave of frustration came over Rex. "Aw, come on!" he grumbled. "Play the game!"

At that moment, Thecla turned and looked straight at Rex. His eyes met hers and he was suddenly, mysteriously, overwhelmed by a feeling he had never experienced before.

Chapter Four

And the Lion Shall Lie Down . . .

Leonie started to pace impatiently in the cage. "Rex! Dear! Just pounce and get it over with!" she called out across the arena. "I'm really rather hungry!"

But Rex didn't seem to hear her. Or, if he did hear, he wasn't listening. Leonie tried again, a little louder this time. "Rex! Why don't you kill the breakfast please! Didn't you hear me?"

Still, Rex didn't move. For what seemed like an eternity, he just stood there, only a few feet away from the breakfast, both of them staring deep into each other's eyes. Leonie was confused.

"What in the world is going on?" she asked herself with a sigh. "Why won't Rex just kill the girl? Here he is, complaining all morning about how hungry he is, and now, *now*, he just stands there like some big, big . . ." But Leonie never finished her sentence. Instead, her mouth dropped open in utter disbelief. There, before her very eyes, Rex did the most incredible, amazing thing she had ever witnessed . . .

He sat down at the lady's feet and began to *lick* her!

A stunned silence fell over the arena, as everyone watched in astonishment. No one dared move, nor speak. Nobody could believe their eyes.

Slowly, Thecla reached out a hand and began to pet Rex, as if he were the gentlest of kittens.

Leonie was frozen to the spot. Was she imagining this? What on earth had come over her husband?

Then, all at once, the crowd seemed to recover from its shock, and everyone started to shout.

"Another lion! Bring another lion!"

"Kill the Christian!"

"Send out the lioness!"

The governor obviously agreed, for he ordered at the top of his lungs, "Release the lioness!"

Before Leonie realized what was happening, the cage door flew open and she was let free. Confused and dismayed, she leapt into the arena and charged at full speed to where Rex and Thecla were peacefully curled up together, cozily side by side.

"Rex! What's the matter with you!" she demanded angrily. This was *so embarrassing*. "You're making an absolute fool of yourself! What's come over you?"

But Rex just sat there, at Thecla's feet, purring contentedly.

Leonie cried out, "Well, if you won't kill the breakfast, *I* will!" And with that, Leonie let out a terrifying roar and lunged at the girl.

Suddenly . . . she stopped.

She didn't know why. It was all so strange and unexpected. An overwhelming feeling came over her, pouring over her like a wave, and for some reason, Leonie was unable to attack the beautiful Thecla! Her impatience, her anger, her ferocity -- they all disappeared. Even her hunger was suddenly gone. Leonie moved as if in a dream. She laid down beside Thecla and, like Rex, began to lick the saint's feet.

Chapter Five

A Little Bird Told Me

It was not till a few days later that Rex and Leonie learned of the beautiful Thecla's fate.

They were basking in the warm sun, as it filtered through the bars of their cage, when suddenly a pigeon landed on the ground outside and began to peck at the dirt.

Rex stood up and went to the bars. "Hey you! Bird!" he called out. "Yeah, *you!* C'mere!"

The pigeon hesitated, afraid of such a big fierce lion.

Rex promised, "I won't hurt you. Come over here. I just wanna ask you something."

The pigeon carefully approached. "What do you want?" he asked, still scared.

"I said I just wanna ask you something," Rex repeated. "Were you here a few days ago when my wife and I were set loose to kill that Christian lady? The one named Thecla?"

"You mean the one you didn't kill?" asked the bird.

Rex nodded. "Yeah. Her."

"Yes," the pigeon answered. "I was here."

"Good," Rex said. "I just wanted to find out what happened to her afterwards. Do you know?"

"Of course I know," the pigeon replied. "Everyone knows. It's all anyone has been talking about for days around here."

Rex was annoyed. "Well *I* don't know, and if I *did* know, I wouldn't be askin' you, would I?"

The pigeon bristled a little, but told him what had happened to Thecla. Leonie came over to listen too as the bird said, "The day after you two were meant to kill her, but didn't, the governor had her tied to wild bulls, so they could drag her to death."

Leonie couldn't help but feel a little sad. "So, Thecla's dead," she said softly.

The bird said excitedly, "Oh no! The ropes mysteriously broke, and the bulls ran away, and Thecla was unharmed."

Rex was impressed. "No kiddin'! How 'bout that!"

Leonie asked, "What did the governor do to her after that?"

"Well," the pigeon replied, "next he had her lowered into a pit of poisonous snakes."

The lions both shuddered and asked together, "And . . .?"

"You guessed it," the bird beamed. "The snakes pulled the same trick you two did, and refused to kill her."

Leonie exclaimed, "Really? You mean, even the snakes wouldn't bite her?"

Rex said, "Now *that's* saying something! Makes me feel like not such a wimp after all."

Leonie was dying to hear the rest. "But then what? What happened next?"

The bird continued the story. "Well, after that, the governor was getting rather scared. A lot of people were beginning to say that the God of the Christian lady was obviously protecting her and that she must be right to believe in Him. So, in the end, the governor decided to let her go."

"Let her go?" Rex repeated, incredulous. "Just like that?"

The bird nodded. "Yep. Just like that. So off she went into the hills to pray, and many people followed her so they could learn about her God and become Christians themselves. And that's all there is to tell, I guess."

Just then, several men came across the arena towards the lions. They had horses, pulling a wagon with a heavy cage on top of it, and the men had long whips. Rex and Leonie glanced at each other with expectation.

Rex said, "Looks like they're going to take us somewhere."

"I wonder why," Leonie said.

"Beats me."

The pigeon shrugged, not knowing why either.

The men arrived and, after a bit of trouble, managed to transfer the two lions into the portable cage and load them onto the wagon.

Then one of the men said, "Back to the jungle for you two, you useless beasts." He shook his head with disgust and added, "What good is a couple of lions who won't even kill a woman? The governor will find a better pair of cats than you two."

The lions couldn't believe their ears! Leonie gasped, "Rex! Did he say *jungle?* They're taking us back to the jungle!!!"

Rex was over the moon. "They're setting us free, Leonie! They're gonna take us home!"

And thus God rewarded the two lions for having spared the life of His faithful servant Thecla.

CUTHBERT FOR BREAKFAST

Chapter One

A Brave New Day for Chester

It was going to be an exciting day. Chester the little goose felt sure of it. Things had gone well for him this past week -- his flying lessons had been getting easier by the day, and now Mother was even allowing him to swim in the pond all by himself with the other young geese. Chester splashed in the cool water, reveling in his newly-found freedom. Reflected in the water he could see the sky, with its cotton-ball clouds drifting lazily across the English countryside. He could see his own reflection too -- his smooth white feathers and sleek neck, and with a touch of pride he thought of what a fine, handsome gander he would make someday. Maybe he would even turn out as handsome as Cuthbert, his older brother!

Suddenly Chester's thoughts were interrupted by a loud splash behind him, and he turned around to see his best friend Delmer doing somersaults in the water.

"Hi-ya, Chester!" Delmer said, coming up for air. "What's up?"

"Oh hi, Delmer. Not much. Just having a swim," Chester replied. "It's the first day Mother has let me come to the pond all alone."

"Me too," said Delmer. "Isn't it neat to finally be growing up?"

Chester sighed wistfully. "I can't wait until I'm as big as my brother Cuthbert. It must be fun to do whatever you want all the time."

"You can say that again," agreed Delmer. "Teenagers sure have it lucky. But, hey, speaking of your brother, there he is, over there on the shore, with Oren and Parry and the others."

Chester looked towards the tall reeds beside the pond where his friend was pointing. Sure enough, there was Cuthbert, surrounded by the whole tough Goose Gang.

"Maybe they will let us join them," Chester said, feeling like doing something exciting today.

But Delmer shook his fluffy head. "I doubt it. They never do. Parry and Oren say we're too little."

It was true. Parry and Oren were bullies. Chester was usually scared of them, but not when Cuthbert was around. Cuthbert was the leader of the Goose Gang, and if he said Chester and Delmer could join them, the other ganders would have no choice but to give in. So, undaunted, little Chester splashed towards the shore and Delmer decided to follow.

"Oh no," moaned Parry, when he spotted the two small goslings heading their way. "Look who's coming. Not those two!" He turned to Cuthbert and demanded, "Tell your baby brother and his friend to get lost. We don't want them over here."

Cuthbert said, "No. Leave them alone. They're allowed on the shore as much as we are."

Chester and Delmer reached the edge of the pond, both breathless from the long swim. It wasn't that far in reality, being only a little pond, but to such small goslings, it seemed a very long way indeed. "May we play with you?" Chester asked hopefully, as he shook the water from his downy wings. "Please?"

Oren stuck his beak haughtily in the air. "Playing is for babies. We're too old for your silly games."

"Go away," Parry said. "We're busy. Can't you see?"

To Chester and Delmer, the big geese didn't look busy at all. They were doing nothing but sitting there in the warm sun. But the whole

Gang started to honk rudely at the two little goslings, trying to chase them away, until Cuthbert ordered angrily, "I said, leave them alone." Cuthbert was the strongest and most handsome of all the young ganders, and everyone knew it. Like it or not, the others always obeyed his commands . . . or else. He was a born leader among geese, both admired and feared by the entire flock. "What do you want, Chester?" he asked his brother.

"Delmer and I feel like doing something exciting today," Chester answered. "We wanted to see if the Gang was doing anything special."

Cuthbert said, "We were just about to go to the Princess's cornfield."

Parry added, "But you two can't come, so don't even ask."

Oren agreed. "It's over a mile away. You're both too puny and useless to fly that far."

"I bet we could!" Delmer said defensively. "We've been practicing flying all week, haven't we, Chester?"

But Chester didn't answer. He was too busy thinking about the cornfield. The cornfield of a *Princess!* Wow! Talk about exciting. "Who is she?" he asked his brother.

"Who's who?"

"The Princess."

Cuthbert said, "Her name is Princess Werburga."

Delmer's eyes got huge. "You mean the daughter of King Wulfere and Queen Ermenhild? I've heard all about her! Some of the horses met her once when they passed her castle. They told me she is beautiful, and super holy too!" He paused, then added, "They say the people call her a saint. What does that mean?"

The geese all looked at each other and shrugged. None of them had a clue what a saint was, but something about the word sounded to Chester breathtakingly wonderful.

"Who cares?" Oren sneered. "It's her *corn* we're interested in, not her. The ravens up the road claim her crop is the most delicious in all of England. We're going to make a raid and find out for ourselves."

Raiding a royal cornfield! Not just any old boring cornfield, but a *royal* one!

Talk about the adventure of a lifetime!

"May we come too?" Chester begged. "Please, Cuthbert? *Pleeeease?* We promise we'll be good!"

"Well . . ." Cuthbert hesitated. "I don't know. Oren's right; it's a long way for you two to fly. And it's going to be dangerous. There's a steward there, some man by the name of Edward, and the ravens warned us he gets awfully mad whenever birds come to steal the Princess's corn. He's always trying to scare animals away."

Trying to frighten Chester and Delmer, Parry added, "He even tried to *kill* a couple of the ravens a few days ago with his bow and arrow. Nearly got them too. One was shot in the wing and barely escaped with his life."

Chester looked at his friend Delmer, suddenly having seconds thoughts. *Big* second thoughts.

A bow and arrow. That sounded, well, scary. Super scary!

"Um . . . maybe we won't go with you after all," Chester said.

But Delmer was getting excited. The fact that it was dangerous made it all the more appealing. "Aw, come on, Chester!" he said. "Are you a goose or a chicken? I say, let's go."

Chester searched for an excuse. He was afraid, but didn't want the others to know. "Mother told me to be back in time for lunch," he said lamely. "It might take too long."

Oren and Parry looked at each other, amused. "Looks like Chester's a chicken after all," Parry said. Then he started jumping around making chicken noises. "Bak- bak! Bak- bak -bak!"

Oren joined him, and so did the rest of the Gang, until all the ganders were pretending to be chickens, hopping and bakking at the top of their voices, making fun of poor little Chester.

"I'm not a chicken!" Chester cried out. "I'm a goose! And someday I'll be just as big and brave as the rest of you!"

"Then prove it!" Parry challenged.

"I will! I'm not afraid to go to Princess Werburga's cornfield! You'll see!"

Cuthbert ordered, "That's enough. Leave him alone." Then he asked his little brother, "Are you sure you and Delmer really want to come? It's a long way, and there won't be any turning back if you change your minds."

Hoping he looked braver than he felt, Chester nodded. Stealing corn was one thing, but bows and arrows were another! Still, he would prove to everyone that he was a courageous goose and not a spineless chicken.

So Cuthbert nodded, spread his graceful wings and took flight.

The rest of the Gang followed, with Chester and Delmer in the rear.

Chapter Two

By Order of the Princess

It wasn't very far, but to the two small goslings the flight seemed endless. They had never flown so far in all their lives, and by the time they finally landed in Princess Werburga's field, their wings ached and their breath was coming in short gasps.

"Are you two alright?" Cuthbert asked.

Panting, Delmer answered, "Yes. It was . . . just . . . a lot farther than . . . we . . . thought."

Parry looked at them with derision. "Told you they wouldn't be able to keep up."

Poor little Chester felt suddenly afraid. He wished he hadn't come. He was exhausted, and wanted nothing more than to be safely back near the old familiar pond, snuggled under his mother's warm, protective wings. But he was determined not to let the ganders see his fear. He glanced up at Cuthbert, and, mercifully, his brother could read his thoughts.

"You two rest here for awhile," Cuthbert said gently to the goslings. "We'll bring you some corn to eat."

That made some of the ganders mad. "Hey!" Oren blurted angrily. "Make them steal their own corn! They're the ones who wanted to come in the first place. We didn't invite them."

"Don't be so hard on them, Oren," Cuthbert said. "They're just babies. Don't you remember what it was like to be a gosling and just learning to fly?"

Oren didn't have the chance to answer, for at that moment they all heard Delmer let out a terrified cry. All the geese turned in time to see a man rushing towards them. He was waving a big stick and his face was red with anger.

"Get away, you stupid birds!" he shouted.

"It must be Edward, the steward!" one of the ganders yelled in panic.

Chester's first instinct was to run! But he was too exhausted . . . and too petrified . . . to move a feather! All he could do was stand there, frozen to the ground, and watch the man with horror.

"Quick! Let's get out of here!" screamed Parry.

All the geese raised their wings, ready to take flight.

But . . . something made them hesitate. To their amazement, Cuthbert was not preparing to fly! He was the leader of the Gang, and if he stayed, they all must! The geese couldn't believe what they were seeing -- instead of flying, Cuthbert was moving to stand between Chester and Delmer.

Then, to Chester's great relief, Cuthbert spread his powerful wings over the two little goslings, hiding them beneath. Shaking and scared, Chester huddled close to his big brother. So did Delmer. They had never been so afraid in their lives.

Edward the steward raised his stick, ready to clobber them. The whole Goose Gang was too frightened to even move. At that moment, they heard a lady's voice call out, "No, Edward! Do not hurt them!"

Everyone looked, and saw a majestic white horse cantering towards them. Atop the graceful mount sat a lady, more beautiful than anyone the geese had ever seen. It must be Princess Werburga herself! She reined in and dismounted in front of Edward and the trembling flock.

"Do not hurt them," she repeated kindly. "They are God's little creatures and have every right to live."

Parry and Oren and the others bristled at being called *little*. They were *big* ganders, anyone could see that!

"But, your Highness," Edward said, "they were about to steal your corn. I was just going to frighten them away."

The beautiful Princess gently shook her head. "Frightening them will do no good, Edward. They will just come back another day, like the ravens do. No, we must teach them a lesson instead."

The steward's mouth dropped open. "Teach them a *lesson*?" he asked with disbelief. "But, my good Princess, they are nothing but brainless *birds!* You can't teach a bird a lesson!"

Well, that made the big ganders fume! Brainless! How dare he call them brainless! Who did this human being think he was?

The Princess said calmly, "They must learn that it is wrong to steal."

The geese all looked at each other, astonished. *Wrong to steal?* But they did it all the time! So did the ravens, and the crows . . . even the rabbits! It was only normal to raid crops.

Edward seemed just as surprised as the Gang. He lowered the stick in his hand obediently and tried not to roll his eyes. "What then, my lady, would you have me do with them?"

Chester felt his heart pounding with fear. He buried himself deeper into Cuthbert's feathers, wishing he could disappear. Then a terrible thought struck him. What if Cuthbert decided to make a run for it after all, and took flight? All the other geese would follow, and he and Delmer would be left here alone, with no escape! Edward would kill them with his big stick! Murder them, in cold blood, just like that!

No, Chester told himself firmly. Cuthbert wouldn't do that to him. He wouldn't abandon his little brother like that.

He realized the Princess was speaking. "Bring these geese into the barn," she was instructing Edward, "and lock them in overnight. I will speak to them myself in the morning."

In his astonishment, poor Edward dropped his stick. "Bring them to the barn? But, truly, my lady! How will I ever get them to follow me?"

Princess Werburga simply smiled and said, "They will. You'll see."

Then she peacefully mounted her horse and rode away.

Edward stood there, dumbfounded, staring at the Gang. The Gang, equally dumbfounded, stared back at Edward. No one knew what to do. Neither man nor bird moved.

Finally Edward shrugged his shoulders. "Okay, geese," he mumbled, "you heard the Princess. Follow me." He headed towards the barn.

The Gang looked at each other helplessly. Then, as if forced by some mysterious power, the entire flock lined up in a neat, tidy row behind Cuthbert – with the two little goslings still under his wings – and started to follow the steward to the barn. No one could understand. It was as if their feet just waddled along behind the man without being able to resist. It was so embarrassing! They felt like a silly pack of puppy dogs at the heels of their master, instead of the wild tough ganders that they were. Even Cuthbert looked confused, but, like the rest of them, he couldn't seem to do a thing about it. He *had* to do what Princess Werburga had said, like it or not. Chester suddenly wondered if maybe it had something to do with her being a *saint*.

If only he knew what that word meant.

Chapter Three

A Terrible Truth . . . A Terrible Day

So off they marched to the barn, where Edward shooed them inside and said, "There, you thieves. No stealing the Princess's corn for you." He was just about to close the barn door and lock them in, when suddenly Chester heard him let out an evil laugh. Then the steward said to himself, "Mind you . . . roast goose don't sound like a bad idea, thinkin' 'bout it! Hmm, I wonder which one of you would be the tastiest."

Before anyone realized what was happening, Edward's strong hand reached out and grabbed Cuthbert by the throat!

The large gander fought back wildly, trying to free himself from the steward's grip. The whole Gang instantly leapt into action, squawking and honking and fighting desperately to rescue their friend. They were pecking fiercely with their sharp beaks at Edward's legs, slapping him with their wings, making such a raucous that the barn was filled with the commotion of battle. But all the birds' efforts

were in vain. The man was too big and strong in comparison with the geese, and all he did was laugh at them.

"Hah! What a fine meal you will make, my friend," he scoffed, carrying Cuthbert by his neck to the door.

"Cuthbert!" Chester cried out in terror. "Do something! Don't let him take you away!"

But it was too late. Edward the Murderer was already outside, with Cuthbert clutched in his evil grip. The barn door slammed shut, and they all heard the sound of the bolt locking it from the other side.

"No!" screamed Chester. "Bring him back! Bring my brother back! Someone do something! Parry! Oren! Save him! *Save him!*" The little gosling flung himself at the door and desperately started to peck at it.

Of all the birds, it was Delmer who bravely spoke. "Don't panic. If we want to rescue him, we have to stay calm." He joined Chester at the door, and both little goslings pecked at its heavy wood with all their strength and all their hearts.

Oren looked at them with disgust and rolled his eyes.

"You stupid little birds," Parry said. "You'll never be able to open that door. Just face it, Cuthbert is as good as dead."

"And it's all your fault," Oren added cruelly. "If you two hadn't come with us in the first place, we'd never be in this mess. It was only because you couldn't fly away that Cuthbert stayed in the cornfield."

Another mean goose joined in. "Cuthbert risked his life to protect you, and now look what's happened to him. He's dead."

"Don't say that!" Chester yelled. "He's not dead! He's not! He's still alive, and we can save him!"

Parry shook his head. "There's no way we can save him, Chester. We're locked in this barn. So stop whimpering like a baby and accept it, will you?"

Accept it?! How could Parry say something like that?

Oren said, "Look, Chester, geese get roasted and eaten all the time. It's a fact of life. It's not pleasant, but, hey, a lot of things aren't. That's just the way things are. So shut your beak and forget about Cuthbert. He's gone, alright?"

NO, it wasn't alright!

"He's my brother!" Chester cried. "I want him back!"

"Well, you won't get him back, runt," another Gang member said. "By now, his neck is snapped in half and he'll soon be simmering in Edward's pot. If he isn't already."

Cuthbert in a pot! The mere thought of it made Chester want to die of sadness. He turned away from the door and tried hard not to burst into tears.

Chapter Four

Trial by Bird, by God Heard

The day lasted forever. It was the most miserable of Chester's life. The barn was dark and stuffy, without even a window to offer the geese a hope of escape. Chester and Delmer were amazed by how little the other birds seemed to care about Cuthbert's coldblooded murder. The big ganders waddled around the barn for awhile, scratching around looking for something to eat, but when they didn't find anything, they fluffed and preened their fine feathers, settled down, and actually went to sleep. *Sleep!* At a time like this! As if Cuthbert had never even existed!

Chester and Delmer huddled together in a corner, as far away from the other geese as possible. They were scared and cold and lonely, and Chester wanted to cry. Finally, worn out by fatigue and hunger, Delmer fell into an exhausted sleep. Beside him, Chester could no longer be brave. The tears started to roll down his soft little face.

He cried himself to sleep.

* * * * * *

The morning at last dawned, and with it came the sound of horses and people outside in the barnyard. At first, when Chester awoke, he wasn't sure where he was. For one blissful moment, he thought he was back at home near the pond, snuggled under his mother's warm feathers. But as his eyes opened and his thoughts cleared, he realized with a sickening feeling that he was snuggled, not against his mother, but against a bale of hay in a dimly lit barn. The events of yesterday came suddenly rushing back to him, and he nearly started crying again. But, no. He knew he had to be brave. It was one thing to cry alone in the darkness of night, cuddled up next to Delmer where the big geese couldn't see him, but another thing altogether to break down in broad daylight, right in front of the whole mean Gang. He couldn't let them see him cry! They would laugh and honk at him, and poor Chester couldn't bear it if they did.

The noises outside were getting closer, and a few minutes later the geese could hear the big barn door being unlocked from the other side.

Chester whispered, "Delmer! Delmer, are you awake?"

Delmer yawned. "I am now," he said.

"Someone's opening the barn door," Chester told him. "Look!"

Delmer sat up and the two little goslings watched with dread as the huge door swung open . . . and in stepped *Edward the Killer!* Chester and Delmer looked at each other and shuddered with fear.

They heard him say, "Well, my lady, here they all are," and he moved aside to let someone enter before him.

It was Princess Werburga herself! At the sight of her kind and gentle face, Chester felt strangely consoled. That word came back to him again. *Saint*. Something about it was so comforting and he felt his little heart start to grow calm.

"Well, my little friends," she said to the flock with a playful smile, "I hope this has taught you all a lesson. It is wrong to try to steal the corn from my fields. Or anyone's fields, for that matter. God will take care of you and feed you, because you are His little creatures and He loves you, but you must understand that stealing is wrong. I trust that now, after a day and a night of being locked up, you will fly away from my farm and return no more. Now, off you go. Away with you."

"Cuthbert! She doesn't know about Cuthbert!" Chester thought. And, before any of the ganders could reach the door, he threw himself in front of it and flapped his little wings frantically, blocking their exit.

"Move out of our way, you little troublemaker," Parry ordered angrily, but Chester made so much commotion that the Princess herself stepped in front of the door, driving the geese back into the barn.

"Wait," she said. "Something is wrong." Bending down, she fixed her kind eyes upon Chester. "Tell me, little gosling, what is it? What is the matter?"

Chester wished desperately that he could speak in human language, but he couldn't. He had no way to tell Princess Werburga about his brother's murder! All he could do was hop up and down and flap his tiny wings in despair. If only – *if only!* – he could let the beautiful Princess know what had happened to Cuthbert, he felt sure she would help him! She was a *saint*, after all! (Whatever that meant.) It seemed so unfair that the cruel Edward should go unpunished for such a terrible crime!

Delmer, too, suddenly seemed to sense the Princess's power to help them, and, racing to Chester's side, he also started to jump around at her feet.

"My goodness," the Princess exclaimed. "Now there are two of you trying to tell me something. You poor little birds. What is it that upsets you so?"

Chester ran over to Edward and started to peck angrily at his legs. If only the Princess could understand!

All of a sudden, to Chester's amazement, Oren dashed over and joined him! "Come on, you guys!" he ordered the rest of the Gang. "Let's all show the Princess how nasty Edward is!"

Instantly, the rest of the flock surged around the dumbfounded steward, honking at him wildly and attacking him with all their might.

Princess Werburga stiffened and turned her gaze to the guilty Edward. "You've done something to upset these geese," she said sternly. "Tell me what it is."

Edward turned pale.

"N-nothing, my lady!" he lied. "I haven't a clue what all this fuss is about."

Chester saw Princess Werburga close her eyes and whisper a prayer. She stood still for a long moment, and then she spoke.

"You are lying, Edward. God, in His goodness, has revealed to me that last night you killed one of the geese, which you ate for breakfast this morning."

Stunned by her words, Edward could not find his voice. He stood speechless.

The Goose Gang stopped attacking him and a hush fell over the barn.

"The Princess *knows*!" Chester whispered to Delmer with awe. Again, that beautiful word, *saint,* came into his mind.

"By what right, Edward," Princess Werburga scolded, "did you take that gander for your meal? He did not belong to you."

Edward stammered, "I . . . well . . . I just thought . . ."

"I wanted to teach these birds that stealing is wrong," the Princess said. "And instead, I find myself having to teach that same lesson to a man who claims to love and serve God." She sighed with sadness. "Go at once and gather the bones, Edward. Bring them here to me."

Edward looked confused. "I beg your pardon, my lady?"

"The gander's bones," she said. "Go get them."

"You mean, *now*?" Edward's face turned red.

"Yes," she said, her gentle eyes still on Chester. "Bring all the bones to the barn. This instant."

Chapter Five

A Brand New Day for Cuthbert

It was a strange mixture of curiosity and hope that held Chester and the other geese spellbound in the barn as they waited for the steward's return. The door was wide open -- they were free to fly away -- and yet, somehow, they felt compelled to stay and see what would happen.

At length Edward came back, looking shameful and bewildered indeed, as he carried a plate of bones and presented them to the Princess. Chester had to look away; he could not bear to see his brother's remains scattered on the rusty old plate like that!

Princess Werburga carefully took the plate and lifted her eyes to Heaven. "Oh God, our loving Father," she prayed, "Thou Who has made all living things, I beg of Thee to restore to life this Thy creature."

Instantly, before their very eyes, everyone saw the bones on the plate lift up and connect together again! Then skin began to grow around them, and finally, beautiful white feathers appeared! Chester

watched, awestruck, as his brother came back to life! Before he knew it, there stood Cuthbert on the plate, as strong and handsome as ever! The geese just stared and stared as Cuthbert calmly jumped to the floor. Edward dropped to his knees in shock in front of the *saint,* and Chester somehow understood what the word meant now.

The Princess gently said to Chester, "You have your brother back, my little friend. Now go, all of you. Return home and steal no more."

Cuthbert bowed before the *saint*, then looked at his little brother with gratitude and love. Wing in wing, they waddled from the barn, then Cuthbert arched his graceful wings and took flight. Chester followed, then the whole Goose Gang.

And they were never seen in the Princess's cornfield again.

*Rex, Leonie, Chester and Cuthbert (and all the Goose Gang)
say good-bye, and hope you meet their friends,
Little Lamb, Joshua, and the Deer, in:*

Animals of God, Volume One

Reproducible

Coloring Pages

These coloring pages may be photocopied

by teachers for classroom use

and by families who have purchased this book.

Please respect copyright law and do not reproduce these pages

for friends or for commercial use. Thank you.

Did you know that reviews help sell books?

If you have enjoyed this book, or others by Susan Peek or Martina Parnelli, please consider posting a brief review on Amazon or Goodreads.

Thank you!

Don't miss Volume One for more stories
of animals who met saints!

About the Author

Susan Peek is a wife, mother of eleven children, and a Third Order Franciscan. Her passion is writing novels of little-known saints and heroes, especially for teens. She is an active member of the Catholic Writers Guild and is currently working on her young adult series, *"God's Forgotten Friends: Lives of Little-known Saints."* Her novels include *"Saint Magnus, The Last Viking,"* which was awarded the Catholic Writers' Guild Seal of Approval and hit #1 Seller for Young Adults on Amazon, *"A Soldier Surrenders"* which has been through four editions and translated into Spanish, and *"Crusader King"*, which was listed among the Top 50 Most Popular Books for Catholic Homeschoolers in 2013. Her books have been implemented into the curriculum of numerous Catholic schools worldwide. *"Animals of God"* is her first series for children.
You can visit her at www.susanpeekauthor.com.

About the Illustrator

Artist and writer Martina Parnelli resides in western Michigan where she enjoys learning about the local flora and teaching the chickadees to eat from her hand. She takes an interest in matters historical and medicinal, as well as all things relating to home craft. As an author, she has written numerous poems, a few stories and several plays. She also enjoys composing music. Her books for children include *"Fat John, His Little Lamb, and the Two Wise Owls"* co-authored with M. Roberto Angelorum and published by Leonine Publishers. She is currently working on *"Little Runty, the Luckiest Donkey,"* the first book of her exciting *Little Runty* series for children.

Made in United States
Troutdale, OR
03/25/2024

18722300R00066